Memories Linked Like Oases

Poetry
Self
Choices
Philosophy
Nature
Love
Politics
Religion
Romance
Time
Aging
and
Death

Duane Vorhees

Hog Press
PO Box 5069
Madison, WI 53705-5069
USA
hogpress.com
editor@hogpress.com
+1 (352) 388-3848
+1 (515) 462-0278

HOG PRESS

MEMORIES LINKED LIKE OASES: Poetry, Self, Choices, Philosophy, Nature, Love, Politics, Religion, Romance, Time, Aging, and Death

2023 © Duane Vorhees

All rights reserved. No part of this work covered by the copyright hereon may be reproduced or used in any form or by any means—graphic, electronic, or mechanical, including photocopying, recording, taping, or information storage and retrieval systems—without written permission of the publisher. Neither the author nor the publisher make any representation, express or implied, with regard to the accuracy of the information contained in this book and cannot accept any legal responsibility or liability for any errors or omissions that may be made.

ISBN-13: 978-1-941892-66-4

Library of Congress Control Number: 2023935965

Book layout and design © 2023 by polytekton
The background of the book cover is a detail of a coat worn by Georges de Selve (Bishop of Lavaur) who is the character on the right in Hals Holbein the Younger's *The Ambassadors* from 1533

Table of Contents

On Reading a Poem for the First Time   9

Fourwords   10
Foil or Fencer   11
Restoring Balances   11
The Certainty of Our World   12
Wind   13

I   14
Mirrors, Heroes, and Seers   15
Edits   16
The Pit   17
Let's Fact It   17
The Mythic Archaic Cub, His Mandala, and Me   18
O Moon   19
Love and Science   20
Kali Yuga   21
Committed   21
The Ajummazation of Rachel*   22
Destinies Shift   24
Scenic   25

II — 26

Malpractice	27
Limits on Infinity	28
Liquidities	29
This Traitor	30
It's All the Fashion	31
Nulla Coitus Eruptus	31
Punctuation: A Friendly User's Guide	32
There is No Dewey System of Governance	34
Making and Naming	35
Pussyfootin' in the City	36
Edging Toward	37
The Postmortem	38

III — 40

In Cohen's Chelsea Hotels	41
"Like a Red, Red Rose"	42
Doubling Through	43
Opiates of the Masses	44
Shadow Monarchs	45
The Harridans Come Riding	46
My Woman is a Rifle	47
Electioneering	48
According to Augustine	49
Tomorrow's Stars [sijo]	50
Tuesday	51
Lulled	52

IV — 54

Insomnia Comes Amnesia Goes	55
Measure Up!	56
Pain is Vast and Torture Stark	57
Fate and Choice	58
Edison Cro-Magnon	59
Winter	60
Luxe, calme et volupté	61
Heroic Transformation	62
Seer, Road, Mirror	63
Your Fault, and Mine	64

Cultivated	65
La ville rose	66

V — 68

memorieslustaddictions	69
The Desired Explanation	70
Ruthless	72
The Geometry of a Point	73
Excerpts from Abelard's Notebook	74
No Rest after Everest	76
Our Wind Our Water	77
Shifting	78
Passio	79
'Till Death Do Us Part	80
Yesterday's Yeast Sore	81
A	
N (*)	
D	
Tomorrow's Tumor	
Where Did the Face of FDR Go?	82

VI — 84

Don't You Remember?	85
Senseless	86
Unrequited	87
Pasticide	88
Limos	89
The Actual Anatomy	90
A Marriage	90
Two Italians Discuss Their Battalions	91
The Fig Leaf Effect	92
30 Years' War	93
Generation	94
Why the Happy Birthday Wishes?	96

VII — 98

Old Soldiers Fade Away	99
Tumblers	100
Age of Ambition	101

What's the Pointillism of It All?	102
Confusion of Perception	103
By Way of Earth and Bone	104
Her Warnings, Her Fate	105
Crane	106
Rainbows and Lightning Bolts	108
Act of Love	110
Quantum Relativity	111
Retired Doesn't Mean Tired Again	112

VIII — 114

Sans entrée	115
A Modest Saga	116
Dawn Children	117
Drive	118
Beware	119
Opposing Octaines: A Diptych	120
Drought	121
Harvest	122
Hope, Love, God	123
Gondwanaland	124
Instant Bristlecone	125
To Be Savored at a Later Date	126

IX — 128

My Lovers, A Puzzle	129
Made to Order	130
My Kireji, My Coke	131
Best Advice I Can Give	132
Brahma and Shiva are the Same	133
Communing	134
Rule Under Law!	135
Come the Revolution	136
The Mare's Breaking In	137
White Dwarf Eulogy	138
Paradoxical, Isn't It?	140
Last Wishes	141

X   142

    Absent Pasts, Mnemonic Futures   143
    Aces and 8s: The Deaths of Poetry   144
    Reflection   145
    Time   146
    Multipledivisionsaremeaningless,existenceremainsone.   147
    Bloom's *Kama Sutra,* new edition   148
    The Firing Squad   149
    Impressario   150
    When They Love Us Not   151
    Crock   152
    After Death, What?   153

Afterwords   154

    A Cento*   155
    Elvis, Oedipus, and Akhnaton   156
    A Dodge City Nativity   157
    Cord for Lifting, For Lynching   158
    The Calligrapher Writes the Landscape   158
    The Parts Left Out May Be as Important as the Parts Left In: An Illustration   159

    About the Author   160

Remembering is not the reexcitation of innumerable fixed, lifeless fragmentary traces. It is an imaginative reconstruction or construction. — Frederic Bartlett

This is a work of poetry and is intended for entertainment purposes only. All characters, letters, numbers, words, and punctuation marks, whether living or dead, are purely fictitious. Any resemblance to reality is strictly coincidental.

On Reading a Poem for the First Time

Relax, It's just like any other text (a page littered with dark insects). Don't try too hard to find a hidden meaning. Just take it for what it is. Maybe there's something about it that appeals to you or makes you respond/think in a certain way. It may not be the way the poet intended, but you can't really know that. Maybe there's nothing special about it, as far as you're concerned (just more black tire marks in the snow). But whether it moves you or not, read another poem some time, or maybe the same one again. Poetry must have something special about it, or we wouldn't have been composing it all these millennia, would we? After you have read enough poetry to be comfortable with its oddness, you can start to examine it for deeper meanings or a closer appreciation of its verbal art. And that way it starts to become your own poem (a slice of moonlight).

Many poems choose to ignore me altogether. Some poems arrive in bra and panties but never get undressed. Some squat wet and naked on my pen, and some even bring a friend or two. Most poems, however, coy eager virgins, need to be encouraged or nurtured or coaxed to discover and reveal themselves.

Every time
the mirror in a compact
opens a new prospect
is primed.

Fourwords

Foil or Fencer

Is breath
in passing
or long lasting—
some waiter,
clerk, or doorman,
or Blessed
Destiny—
not happenstance
but weightier,
like the Lord's hand?
Is death
instrument
or the agent—
a rapier
or the swordsman?

Restoring Balances

"The sky is less firm than the earth,"
you said. "Populate the heavens
with staid, dependable ravens
that will outweigh the birds of mirth."

I swallowed a brace of black stones
to add gravity to my soul,
but levity hid in my bones
and mischief outrobined your crows.

The Certainty of Our World

We perceive existence squintingly.
In one moment our desert
becomes a blizzard.
We shelter in a treasure cave
and then see it's a grave
and the celadon bowl
we drank from is someone's skull.
We close our eyes, clear our minds,
once more find ourselves in the mine.
And the ground on which we stand—
it's Waikiki sand and it's quicksand
and then back again but now it's rock
or we're swaying on a stormy dock.
Opposites may all be true at once
or equally false and unfixed. All depends
on distance, circumstance, and our senses.
Ready for the drought
we discover the flood.

Wind

Because Mankind thinks
we are made of flint
we like to yoke
windflow to hope
and freedom,
but, really, the wind
is just the earth breathing.
And Mankind, witless
as kittens,
hides from thunder,
not knowing
it's only
the world's laughter.

I

Mirrors, Heroes, and Seers

Every future remakes its pasts
to meet its present needs.

Historical records
are lost or found
are interpreted
are redacted
are ignored
are invented
are deleted
to create
a collective
suitable memory.

My inner chronicler
collaborates with
my inner seer
to recast
Bystander
as Hero
as Villain
as Victim
as Martyr
reflecting
that moment's
psychic mirror.

Edits

The world began as a poem.

The carping stars perused and demanded change:
stanzas altered or deleted, periods collapsed,
crust hardened, axes tilted,
poles reversed, landmass sent adrift.

Mountains became oceans, and glaciers plains.
Form after form went extinct.
"What good is stegosaurus, anyway?"
"Isn't Neanderthal redundant?"

When stars tired of bickering over biota and commas
they assigned scrivener mankind to recompose.

The Pit

Auditioning for my cock fight
(one of those meticulous rites)
I earned compliments and complaints
from my fellow scoundrels and saints.

A sacristan prepared my spurs
to assuage his superiors,
(not all of them smothered their laugh)
and the presbyters blessed my gaffs.

We each took our turn in the pit,
strutting about, crowing a bit,
to elicit the world's applause,
flourishing ferocious wings, claws...

and (judged to be weak or potent)
who to be culled and who chosen).
our names were entered in some list.

And then, like that! we were dismissed.

Let's Fact It

Sex is lacking in creativity,
like math and bad poetry,
but how many figures have been consumed,
how many rhymes entombed,
in its quaint pursuit.

The Mythic Archaic Cub, His Mandala, and Me

I wait here still for the wise old man
and his chatter of universal traits,
how they shape my acts like hands
on a potter's wheel (but hereditary, innate).

"Archetypes are to psychology
as instincts to biology."

I sit in his psyche, peeling my mandarins,
and wonder, is this a proper asana?
Some tables down someone strums a red mandolin
and my self stifles respondent hosannas.

My me was always confused by my we,
and I was never the one I used to be.

I used to take my tea with cream
but now I prefer lemon.
Why do I have all these dreams
about so many different women?

Decades have crossed like clouds over seas
as I search for any convenient lee.

The minutes pass like birds in flight
and my shadow cowers in shadows
I interpret as monstrous daytime nights.
Mandolinist fingers dissolve into adders.

O Moon

Shakespeare was too polite calling you inconstant.
You'll flash your waxed silver clit for anyone.
Your fabled vagina spawns the stars and poems
but when I most need you to arouse,
you hide, as though demure.

Love and Science

Wasn't it Einstein
who gave precision
to relativity?
They say a life without love is a cataclysm.
Why didn't Einstein
make love
less variable?

Wasn't it Newton
who took force
from an apple?
The first discovery of love is like baptism.
Why couldn't Newton
delineate
passion's energy?

Wasn't it Fleming
who wrested the cure
from the mold?
The loss of ardor is psychic catastrophe.
Did Fleming know
there is no relief
from lust?

Didn't Einstein
define love as
space, time, and power?
The persistence of such love is a masterpiece.
Didn't he actually posit Eros
as mutual carnality squared?

Kali Yuga

Gone is the age of terror and despair
(of bombs and the burnings) —
Now is the age of mystery and conspiracies
(a time of Gordian intricacies).
Painterly, we await
an age of perception and simplicity
(of orange and olive trees).

Committed

We're committed by prayer,
we're committed by crime,
committed to pursuit
of the blood and the wine.

Some cells are filled with monks,
and some are filled with cons.
Some of us are lifers
and some are hangerson.

The Ajummazation of Rachel*

Her social role's yoke was too heavy,
like gold coins under the oaken tree.
She neglected the seed of her freedom,
honoring the ajumoni creed
to acquire approvedof family.

Music was her suitor when we met.
She hoped it would assist her escape
from knots and coils of tradition nets,
though she dreaded she was trapped by fate.

I swore that I'd be her gardener
and I'd nourish her into full bloom.
I shared the Tale of the Pardoner
as we philosophized in my room.

I introduced her to rum cola
(she liked to call it libido juice).
She fingered and bowed her viola,
I discovered how human its voice.

And we practiced our perfect duet.
Oh, how like a viola she'd sound!
We'd beach amidst our salt and our sweat,
clutching like the lifeguard and the drowned.

And so I took her in, to teach her
my lessons of love and liberty.
But when she was no more a seeker,
she dropped me, just short of her degree.

The social role's yoke was too heavy,
like gold coins under the oaken tree.
She abandoned the seed of her freedom
as she filled the ajumoni need
to achieve approvedof family.

As waves of other futures roll by,
I hope she's consoled by her music.
And now at last, when tears have run dry,
string quartets just make me nostalgic.

* Ajumma is a Korean term for a married (or middle-aged) woman, separate from a young unmarried woman and a grandmother. Traditionally, she assumes all household responsibilities, including status-preservation.

Destinies Shift

Like a detective or salesman after a lead,
a jealous extra hungry for the first lead role,
my destinies shift between control and rolled dice.

Knowing the sea will be not forever ice free
along my chosen route, do I want to freeboot
or aspire to engage as a cruise ship boot black
and watch the unsettled play their slots and black jack
in quest of their elusive holy grail jack pot
while jaded doves adrenalize in the spot light?

The isolated, stark figure of the light house
confronts the image of the softbobbing house boat
like a cradle rocking itself in its boat slip
moored oh so serenely by its careful slip knot
which is not (not!) a noose. It's a kind of knot ring.

O, to be barefoot beach boy, heedless of ring worm.

Scenic

Yesterday I was an open field,
cosmosfilled.
Distant horizons misted in all directions.
The face of the earlysummer sun wore its smilingeveryday forecast.
(You said the sight of my noontime sundial always made you blush and giggle.)
And the wind combed through my hair and through the chickadees' pinions.
I had many solstices ahead.

Today I am a closed airless room.
(You insisted you got bored winding my grandfathers clock.)
The vases are empty, the dark curtains drawn against winter's albino glare,
and the hair and the parakeets molted long ago.
I've left many solstices behind.

Tomorrow soon I'll be an ocean.

II

Malpractice

The ambulances full of years have passed.
Yet dependent on drugs, crutches, and slings,
my condition continues to get worse.

I still carry some fragments of our past.
Plagued by the bad, I forget our good things.
Time was my doctor, Amnesia my nurse.

Limits on Infinity

Some poets commend rhymes as maps
that determine direction

and establish borders
to give their poems order.

With the same assessment,
others condemn rhymes as traps.

Liquidities

In command of schedule and lipstick,
the executive goes electric
as she manipulates her firm liquid,
a fiscal mix of stone and stick.

She's nixed by the whiskey mystic
as he listens for his cosmic fix.
The mystic exists amidst the unbrick.

This Traitor

Where I grew up
no one had a future,
no one a past.
The alarm cocks
signaled their whens
that a stalwart
was on the way
to supplant that
adventurous one,
that traitor!, who
had decamped
in the night.

Oh, how in my mind
I rehearsed that sun.

It's All the Fashion

After
arousing passion,
slaughter.

Nulla Coitus Eruptus

Lavayearning Vesuvius
in harlot satins,
loverburning,
lascivious for scarlet bedrooms.

Punctuation: A Friendly User's Guide

A quarter hour's seadriven rain
and craterlets pock sand
like a scholarful of . . .
in an academic's body of work

Then in sunlight's return
they're augmented
by a new bevyworth
of bellybuttons
yours among the many

Familiar gawkers who think
they well know your . dismiss it
as just another in the crowded
ubiquity of quotidian endings
no more remarkable
than the (and the)
that frame your face
or the , , of your nostrils

But this devoted grammarian
of your exquisite style —
I hold your . in the highest regard
as treasure excavation's end and start
Off from the bloated seashore
twin !! demarcate safety's reach
the buoys rise and bounce
heave and sway
in rhythm with nature's swells

Of the many determined hardy swimmers
only a few exhausted by the effort
have ever managed to grope
those floating globes
or stroke them for good fortune
in the fervidly imagined journey ahead

None have reached boundary markers
as often as I but—never one
to tarry on the familiar—
after making proper obeisance
to the !!'s holy role
always I knew I must brave again
the dark open ocean below
or else lose my place ashore

After all my desperate departures
even when most deeply explored
your ? has kept its mystery renewed

And when with my remnant strength
I then manage to dogpaddle back
from your stillsecret ? so
my grateful fingers may sleep
on the landscape of your .

There is No Dewey System of Governance

Do not confuse the falcons with the doves.
All rulers govern by fraud, by force.
Yes, librarians do organize — but books, not power.
It is the bibliophobes — barbarians —
who are in charge, and their conning allies
(the ones we call parliamentarians)
who write the lawbook in their favor (they call it justice)
while dressing raptors in silver quills.

Making and Naming

The All was made
by the Singular Many
in less than a week,
but Man is still finding names
so many years later.
Maybe this is because
from the Tree of Knowledge
shame could have been derived
by Man only.

Pussyfootin' in the City

All those nights my testosterone howled,
amped up by incessant commercial lectures,
I hunted my muchhyped rapture.
But I felt dwarfed by architecture
and isolated within the crowd.

*(The average penis is some 5 inches long;
multiply by the city's male population.)*

I once courted a turner
and imagined contorting together,
gliding and sliding ourselves against gravity
before landing on our feet.
But she refrained due to twisties.

*(The rubber band vagina, also 5 inches deep,
may expand to seven.
Multiply by the number of women.)*

And then there was that diver,
so inviting in her mask and leather.
I pictured us slipping and dipping in liquid,
barely taking time to breathe.
But always she would plead the bends.

*(Subtract one genital total from the other
to find the sex desperation index
measured in pussy feet.)*

Edging Toward

Adulthood is the slowdying stage, the lifecycle's adulteration of youth: carnivorous years gorging at our carnival. Discipline and mercy are not bestowed by disciple or mercenary — we compose ourselves, from the heap of our own compost.

The Postmortem

Your doom and your disappearance
are but two of death's deceptions.

You won't ride with the valkyries
or be serviced by sweet houris.

Don't expect balance and feather,
an accounting in a ledger,
an inquisition by angels,
the companionship of sages.

You'll have no Hell/karma/Heaven—
judgment's privileged to the living.

Your remains are genes and atoms,
and memories are your statues.

III

In Cohen's Chelsea Hotels

Your body, picked and fingered;
old melody newexplored,
lyrics brutal yet tender
through a progression of chords,
wrist atwist like a tumbler.
Lover lost but rarely mourned,
your faint sweet fragrance lingers.
Love cannot ever be learned.
Love is only remembered.

"Like a Red, Red Rose"

Pandora gave mankind meaning
though camouflaged as woe.
When Homer invented simile
he was like a living poem
seeding generations.
Unlike that first woman, however,
these perennials exposed the hope.

Doubling Through

the eating and the eaten
the rower and the drowned
we play our headsup poker
under alldaybreakfast sky
solar yolk and lunar white
the cosmic egg is broken
my IQ is an ice cube

while i consume my whiskey
and my packs of cigarettes
my cigarettes and whiskey
are active consuming me

Opiates of the Masses

Crucifiction, Failosophy, Hisstory:
Tomorrow is a myth. And so is yesterday. Now is all.
Physicks, Asstrology, Isometricks:
Yourself, as you are at present, is your only guide.
Medisin, Accupunkture, Sighchiatry:
There is no cure for reality.
Litterature, Statuwary, Musick:
Art is a grand mirage that takes great pride in being so.
Soshellism, Dicktatorship, Demockracy:
All government systems are synonyms for slavery.
Kingdumbs, Milittearism, Onerousship:
Allegiance to others is suicide.
Noosepapers, Liebraries, Educashun:
"Knowledge" socalled is mere pretense.
Relashunships, Guarantease, Freedumb:
Promises are illusions. But illusions may also be promises.
Ambishun, Suckcess, Sellebrity:
Selfpromotion is the greatest deception of all.
Syphillisation:
Truth is what you trust.

Shadow Monarchs

Courage is not just the medal, and love not the ring.
Our identities transcend our organs, nerves, and bones.
No ideas, no concepts, are ever concrete things,
and neither are those handsome words by which they are known.
The world we see is made of steel, stone, plastic, glass, wood,
material structures made of molecules, atoms,
nucleons, hadrons, quarks, firmions, and other Coulds
and Shoulds (names await definition of a datum).
We preside over realms of rebars and 2x4s
but we're subjects of shadow monarchs called metaphors.

The Harridans Come Riding

The Harridans come riding,
Their quiet white hair jagged,
miming their pennants of lightning.

Beware these bold frenzied hags
when they blow their thunder horns,
when they unfurl their tempest flags.

The Harridans come riding
on hammering black stallions,
quick, relentless, lifting, diving.

Boats are swallowed, sailors lost,
eternal coastlines altered,
and turtles, whales, and seagulls tossed.

Brave landlubbers, go hiding,
light your candles, say your prayers
when the Harridans come riding.

My Woman is a Rifle

The dusty sun gallops to a conclusion,
the wind rehearses the coyote's cry.
And I ride weary homeward
where my upright woman stands,
cold and blue, in the corner.
She is waiting
for my cock and finger,
to catch fire.

I'm no goddamn extension
of anyone's personal pronoun,
no phallic metaphor.
Hot and uncornered,
I belong to myself alone.
The wind should just shush,
and the sun can stay in its place
for all I care.
Despite the fantasy factory
of your belief,
I'll go off
when I'm ready.

Electioneering

We pigeons
coo and nod on
the raven's
coy oration.

According to Augustine

I don't know if I believe
or don't believe in free
will, but I do know it's cheap.
Going on social media
or watching any TV
station is all I need.

Tomorrow's Stars
[sijo]

Your lips invited, mine complied — with their embrace, courtship commenced.
Disheveled petals marked the event. Afterwards, the stars —
they still promised tomorrow, but their distance they retained.

Tuesday

The silence turns to wind.
The newborn becomes a sigh.
Every anniversary's a sword in the blood.

Lulled

By the shine of my headlights
that wolf that hides by the roadside
is simplified to only eyes.
The bright ahead
lets me forget
how black's the edge.

IV

Insomnia Comes Amnesia Goes

There's no echo of the aches,
no fracture, no track, no wake.
Remembrances hibernate.

Is a razor blade
a razor blade yet
once it's lost its edge?

If wounds made no mark,
slicings left no scars,
did the cuts occur?

No memory sleeps alone
but shares its bed with dozens
whom you think are forgotten.

Measure Up!

Let your truths be sung
through your soulwar
disasters,
standoffs, and defeats.
Remodel your tongues.

Poets of yore
were masters
of meters and feet.

Ivy's come unhung
from your towers,
Prose bastards
puke on form, they eat
each other's loose dung.
Their quick manure
jackhammers
legacy concrete.

Rebuild, stone by stone—
and walls, reflower.
Retravel
venerable streets.

Pain is Vast and Torture Stark

I bleed for danger, damn it!
All my stars
are still and dark.
My sun's black,
moon's craterscarred.
I need to change my planet.
Give me crack
and threeeyed jacks,
a fast car,
plenty of gas
to seek out stranger habits.

Fate and Choice

My fellow knaves and wenches
—and saints, knights, and laureates too—

relieve your wrath and tensions
at the city park near you.

Listen to jazzy finches,
throw a frisbee, read a book,

choose among the paths and benches
that determine our life's look—

benches that accord us rest
on the paths that fix our quest.

Edison Cro-Magnon

Our pleasure fathers progress:
Someone created the Ball

but the players had no time
so then invented the Wheel

(but hard playing led to thirst
which thus suggested the Bowl)

and augmented games later
with the Balloon and the Bell.

Winter

Throughout this, our hinterland,
the fractured years are splintered
into climates and seasons.

Implacable divisions
permeate our existence
with successes, bereavements,
curses, and beatitudes.

But it is with certitude
that we honor our Winters
as among the most bitter.

We do so with good reason.
Winter is the raw lesion
between the lifetime essence:
birth, growth, and death. Repentance
ends fall's pains, spring's gratitude
across zones and latitudes.

Luxe, calme et volupté

Love letters,
urgent and clear
—a lifesaver 's whistle—
your kisses in my ears,
whispered epistles.

Your fingers
furrow my follicles.
The seismograph
of my skin
reacts.

I practice
spinalchord
love songs
along your
keyboard vertebrae.

Picnic follows tease.
We sandwich
ourselves with
mayonnaise
and pickle.

Heroic Transformation

The closing of the door provides the key.
Bullets secured the Gandhis and the King,
as Joan of Arc transcended the burning.
The blade for Ali, the ax for Trotsky.
For William Wallace, the rope and quartering.
There can't be Socrates, without hemlock,
or a Jesus the Christ without a cross.

Seer, Road, Mirror

The seer strode the highest road
with a clearbright mirror on his back.
He twitched and he turned
and twisted to discern
the unseen visions that rode his back,
the heroes, virgins, demons, dragons
of the world. And though the glass showed
all the mountains, the mud, and the heavens,
the image was backwards and always flawed.

Your Fault, and Mine

I live an unlaughable comedy,
confined within an imperfect sonnet.
I unravel motley as I don it —
as though nakedness were a remedy.
But I can never detach self from frock
and can't unwear my uniform of rags.

I know you'll refuse to salute my flag.
You can't distinguish the hen from the hawk.
And yet, you say you'll praise any marquis
after all, or some other personage;
the title makes him a man of knowledge
and certainly not an ape of caprice.

Despite your lack of discrimination
I can't bear the thought of separation.

Cultivated

The dappled divided lives we lead.

Between the ordered orchard of science
and the tangled arbor of conscience,
if we're not serving the apple of our gravity
we're serving the apple of our sin.

La ville rose

You know you've gotten old when you prefer the massage to the masseuse.
From pesto New York you've moved, like Monod, to adagio Toulouse.
Now, trapped in your doomed ancient town between barrage and surrender's
        truce,
how your quaint Pink City lodgings turn to puce.
Your vision constricts. You can focus on a corsage but not the spruce.
You have left only one category of triage when in the noose

V

memorieslustaddictions

fireworks flowers dormant in deserts
empty bustiers blushing in closests

trespassed winter in spring's jurisdiction

obachan shadows on groundzero walls
boney clappers begging in hungry bells

anomiedustafflictions
sympathytrustaffection

The Desired Explanation
— Geraldus Cambrensis on Poets and Readers; Lewis Thorpe tr (a found poem)
with a Cywydd Dewair Fyri commentary

"They roar out violently,
are rendered beside themselves,
and become
(as it were)
possessed by a spirit.

"They don't deliver
the answer
in a connected manner.

"But the person
who skillfully observes them
will find

"—after many preambles
(and many nugatory
and incoherent
though ornamented
speeches)—

"the desired explanation
conveyed
in some turn of a word.

"These gifts
are usually conferred
upon them in dreams.

"Some seem to have
sweet milk
or honey
poured on their lips.

"Others fancy that
a written schedule
is applied
to their mouths."

The two dragons' shrieks wreaked the rue
of all those whom their noise sliced through.
The Red Dragon won after wine
led to their entombment as swine.
A verse that roars soars over souls,
overshoots its mark, fails to foal;
it intends to strike like bright light
on shadow, but just extends night.
But verse that whispers cures and corns—
it gives birth, preserves, inspires, mourns.
The worth it instills builds and bonds
our souls to all those lives we don.

Ruthless

In the Hard Times
of my checkered past
I played ruthless checkers.

Now I'm doing hard time
in punishment for getting kinged,
and the Warden whets the guillotine.

The Geometry of a Point

Give me a blind old designer
and a rainbow of grays.

A movie of the grooves of a record
playing some monotone symphony.

A wort-only horticulture.
No infinity beyond one.

A predictive deity,
a singular oddnumbered god.

Because change is so dangerous.

Excerpts from Abelard's Notebook

I knew words never demonstrate the truth in things,
they are just sounds we use for our own convenience,
but when I chose my name with careful confusion,
showing off by punning in Latin, German, and Hebrew
to connote and conflate my noble ability's (*hevel*'s)
dance (*ballare*) with steadfast vanity (*hevel* again),
I knew, of course, *hevel* was the name of doomed Abel,
but I failed to realize it as being cognate to empty, fleeting, breath —
the breath that you, dear Heloise, someday some night
would steal with your spices when your lips would split —
I failed to appreciate that your apple (another pun, oh dear!),
like that of Eve the mother of that Abel,
would be indeed that tender, blossoming tree
to which (from which) I'd cleave.
And who could know the man who'd write "Dull is the Star"
to you, to you, would (still in misplaced youthful jest)
dub our son Astrolabe in hopes he'd identify infinity?
Oh, what was I thinking? Despite what the people and the Church
do say, our Astrolabe truly cannot be illegitimate in God's eye.

In the words of a wise but misunderstood "heretic,"
one you know all too well,
logic, it is true, made me hated in the world,
a vagabond and a fugitive tormented without end,
a string of calamities unbroken to the present day,
like a fire which fills the hall with smoke but no light,
I suffer more from the scandal than from the scar.

I explained to the bleating unheeding tonsured horde
that Doubt begat the Skeptic, and the Skeptic
begat Inquisition, the father of Truth.
And understandings are the offspring of Abstraction,
and understanding requires three qualities:
Sola (alone), separate from the senses,
and *Nuda* (bare), unadorned by prejudgment,
and *Pura*, without adulteration.
And thus, God is known by logic and emotion.
But in my pride and zeal I neglected *Sola*
and married my *Pura* and my *Nuda*.
Et le coq inspecté les oeufs dans ta poulailler,
as I used to say in those less docile days
before the caponization.

We achieve pleasure because God made us in such a way.
Nature has made pleasure a human necessity.
Who can blame a tired hungry monk who lies down
in a soft warm bed that holds a comfortable woman?
We can be compelled to want what we do not want to want
and we must, after all, be judged by intent, not just action.
I taught that happiness is a mental tranquility
brought about by attaining grace and virtue,
but I confess, O Heloise, my own greatest happiness
was when my priest was active in your cloister.
I guess even a flaccid man may still have a tumescent mind.

I don't know.

No Rest after Everest

The challenge is strongest at the mountain's base, not its peak.
But, oh! the climb!
The thin invisible air on the treacherous slopes,
the uncertain sherpas,
The shortness of breath and the tallness of the fear of
fal
ling
to the valley's belly far below.
And then the summit.
The camera captures the skyraised fist, the fluttering standard beside.
A final upswell of the breast
and then begins the long
d
 e
  s
   c
  e
    n
      t

Our Wind Our Water

And now we're fixed in place at last
and, with our futures, tethered fast.
You spent your time trying to outrun the rain,
I tried staying centered in my hurricane.
When the waters caught you I drowned
and winds that found me forced you down.

Shifting

Behold the red and the black smiths,
masters of the bold House of Ink,
as uncalloused fists lose their grip,
undone by the arts of the pink.

Passio

I knew from my earliest youth
my destiny to be a martyr,
so I majored in high abuse,
and promptly rehearsed my stigmata.

When my ambition came unloosed
and I lost my consuming ardor
for fire, for stone, for ax, for noose,
Via Dolorosa got harder.

To put my schooling to good use
I opted to become an author.

'Till Death Do Us Part

In the chapel
we bowed and prayed
to spend our lives together
like the dapple
details the glade.

We spend our time together
like a scalpel
and hand grenade.

We rend our life together,
survive shrapnel
and tempered blade
and bend our ties together.

Between
Yesterday's Yeast Sore
A
N   (*   )
D
Tomorrow's Tumor

(* Books read or neglected, gods worshiped or ditched, roads traversed or abandoned, loves or hatreds embraced. Lovers meet, a part of them do part. Couples couple, births are berthed, babies babied, kids kidded; adults are adulterers or not. Some people die, some are never born. And life is lived with only tears and laughter left.)

Where Did the Face of FDR Go?

I found a dime
by the railroad track.
It was old and gray
bent, dull,
worthless.
The tail was battered,
the head worn and blank.
We were minted
the same year.

VI

Don't You Remember?

antigrav daydream swimming
timeless buzzbrain grins
rhymes of elusive elucidation
and dizzying distraction —
isn't that what being in love was like?

And, alas, time's the effective scrubber
of that festive infestation.

Senseless

A poet must be insensitive
—blind enough to see the world
The rabbi may read the Qur'an
—deaf enough to hear its soul
and the Pope, the Upanishads
—distasteful enough to sweeten life
—unfeeling enough to touch a foreign mind
and yet will bless the war on
humans' love for other gods.
—and anosmic enough to smell truth's decay.

Unrequited

I know you imagined I was strong
but you failed to notice I am straw.

You wanted me to show you the Way
but my lighthouse was but one more wave
in a vast and dark moonridden sea.

And then you desired I'd be the seed
that would build us a tree bold and true
but all we left was another truce.

How can fodder ever hope to win,
subject to the whims of fire and wind?

Pasticide

Dawn opens with a wrathful reveille.
(rats and gnats and vampire bats)
It wakes my ghostly hosts of reverie.
(eagles and sharks and harpies)
Each sunrise haunts me with thoughts of whatif
(reptiles, raptors, piranhas)
and seals me, whipped and torn, into pain's pit,
(vultures and tarantulas)

The daybreak is broken by memory
(dire wolves, tigers, and spiders)
of friends betrayed, life commitments delayed,
(leaches, leopards, and lions)
unjust old grudges without remedy.
(panthers, pythons, scorpions)
Today is just another yesterday.
(hornets, grizzlies, and gators)

Every breakfast consists of pain and ache.
(orcs, falcons, and tsetse flies)
Not even noon provides any relief.
(razorbacks and sabertooths)
No daylight thief can ever steal my grief.
(jackals, crocks, and cancer)
So I await an eternal daybrake.

I know the pain results from my pride,
and pleading priests promise peace can find me,
but I can't repent or take the knee.
It's not possible to apologize.
(wolverines, bees, mosquitoes,
fire ants, and barracudas...)

Limos

With her hardball knees
and basketball abdomen—
Hunger never plays

The Greeks knew Hunger well,
daughter of Discord, sister of Ruin.
An amalgamation of bloat and emaciation,
she once inhabited Aethon's innards
to make him devour himself from within.

But the Greeks knew Prometheus too.
He gave men writing, math, agriculture,
he gave them fire, and even restored
the hope his sister had withheld.
All to keep Hunger, insatiable Hunger, at bay.

Hunger's bony snowshoe feet
bear her shambling ramshackle corpse,
spindly jolly roger crucifix protruding.
Her empty burlap tits hang from pegs,
her skin a crisp parchment
lettered by visible veins,
tightly bound to volumes of bones.
Her cracked and crusted lips
mouth equations of halitosis and dust.
Her cheeks sprawl like abandoned adzes,
her nose a rusted plow.
The ashes of apathy show from mineshaft eyes
after an unremembered fire
consumed whatever was left of hope.

The Greeks knew, of course,
that Prometheus would be
punished for impertinence,
fettered on Hunger's barren mountain,
Aethon dining on his liver.

The Actual Anatomy

Well, in medical terms,
the brain is superior to the shoulder
(also, in social terms,
and not only among the status holders).
But, though the brain may learn,
without the muscle it can't move a boulder.

And, in medical terms,
the shoulder is superior to the heart,
but not in social terms
since people believe hearts center love and art.

And, in medical terms,
the heart is superior to genitals,
but not in social terms:
in art — thought — love — passion is fundamental.

A Marriage

The names on the jerseys
are the same as last season
but the players inside
have changed.

Two Italians Discuss Their Battalions

"How many does the pope have?" asked Bonaparte, making zeroes with his hands. Chiaramonti, snapping his fingers, piously replied, "Those legions, they are invisible and indivisible."
So Chiaramonti held his breath, held his tongue, and crowned l'Empereur.
In gratitude, Napoleon, with hands still full of 0s, took Roma for himself and imprisoned the pontiff.
But when the Empire collapsed, Pius enjoyed a long fingersnapping peace on Earth (or at least in the Vatican), and Napoleone di Buonaparte was exiled to Elba so he could expound on divisions and other matters to his heart's content, and in his native Corsu! Pius sent him a confessor.

[Note to Stalinists: This is a poem, not a treatise on history.]

The Fig Leaf Effect

All in awe, we Adams in the audience
sat in the pondside forest morn
while curtains parted and lights came up.
The pristine performer stood on stage
as naked as Eve after our costectomy.
The robin's peachy breast swayed
to the playful slow rhythm of her bobbing head,
moved by the silent dawn chorus of suitors,
her titties waves along a shore.
Peering at her captive mirror (our eyes)
and smiling like a microscope, she flourished her hair
and we gripped armrests and twisted in our pants.
Our tongues and lips tasted of desert.
With practiced brushes and knowing pencils,
with careful paint and trusty powder,
and a splash of faithful vinegar and water,
she Audoboned her robintohawk camouflage.
covered her upper brown part with a confusion
of sequins and satins, her white undertail coverts
with a thunderous rainbow rag, her whitish belly
with a surefire belligerence flag.
She serpentslithered into a shapeshifter condom,
imprisoned her brown feet in black iron maidens,
and flew, triumphantly, into the wings. And back in
Eden, all that applauding AdamAdamAdam wanted
was the chance to undress her again.

30 Years' War

I mistook silence for license,
beginning our war of attrition.
I multiplied my divisions,
you withdrew and withdrew
behind towers and minefields
(addictions, subtractions).
The assault against inaction
saw stalemate not ceasefire.

Generation

Cicadas once were humans whom Muses gifted with ceaseless song, causing them to starve to death, but only to resurrect resurrect resurrect.

Where families once sacrificed to Poseidoneptunus, they now pay obeisance to Allah or to Elohim aliases. Marduk, Mars, and Quetzalcoatl are no more. What happened to Picts, Pequots, Etruscans, Rozvi? And who answers to inca,kaiser,shahanshah?

Dweller of Bilad arRafidayn— are your Sumer taxes in arrears?

Dem bones, dem bones, dem dry bones
Dem bones, dem bones, dem dry bones
Dem bones, dem bones, dem dry bones
Now hear the word of the lord.

Sumer destructed by Akkadia
Akkadia destructed by Cyrus
Cyrus destructed by Alexander
Alexander destructed by Seleucids

Seleucids destructed by Parthia
Parthia destructed by Sassanids
Sassanids destructed by caliphates
(Rashidian, Umayyad, Abbasid)

Caliphate destructed by Mongols
Mongols destructed by Jalayirids
Jalayirids destructed by Black Sheep
Black Sheep destructed by White Sheep

White Sheep destructed by Safavids
Safavids destructed by Ottomans
Ottomans destructed by British
I hear the word of the lord.

Dem bones, dem bones, dem dry bones
Dem bones, dem bones, dem dry bones
Dem bones, dem bones, dem dry bones
Now hear the word of the lord.

Dem bones, dem bones, gonna rise again?
Dem bones, dem bones, gonna rise again?
Dem bones, dem bones, gonna rise again?
I hear the word of the lord

That future that always matters most resides in some few square centimeters of skin. All else, no matter how loud, no matter how gaudy or insistent, is as extraneous as cicadas.

Why the Happy Birthday Wishes?

My old corpus consists of the gaps
caused by lost companions.
The Fortress reverts to sand,
the Library to pith and pulp.
The battle flag's a bumper sticker now.

Sorely tested before, the Monk's test celibacies
are threatened no more by the Monk's own testes,
my sole components that sleep in peace.

Yesterday's Lion is today's singapura,
and my former Stallion a burro.
But Buddha and Shakespeare
died on their birthdays,
so I look forward to the morrow..

VII

Old Soldiers Fade Away

Memories — my dear comrades of old
(The fire we braved!
And the rations and the women
we shared!) — you've renounced
your rank and distinction.

Still attached to my boots
but you shirk in the rear.
You have become shadows
who conspire behind my back
to disappear in the shade
and camouflage your remnant connections
to all our wars, our occupations,
the exercises and commendations
that shaped my life's deployment.

Tumblers

In this world that rewards the nimble people
the agile poets aspire to be clumsy.
Below the glitter city' spires and steeples,
they keep their lazarettos clear and humble.
To enroll in the Grand Order of Cripples
we first must let our feet teach us to stumble.

Age of Ambition

When I was a youngyoung man
I was borne on the shoulders
of triumphant tomorrows.
Crowds cheered my trophies and rings.

I ran with a golden horde
when I was an oldyoung man.
We believed our zodiacs
and in the bright future flame.

Through the fractures and debris
that remained from our thinned grade,
when I was a youngold man
I shouldered my weary way.

I limp and stumble alone.
The inertia of my intent
bears me toward dim glory
now that I'm an oldold man.

What's the Pointillism of It All?

The dotted bourgeoisie are dressed in their careful *dimanche* best
So as to be seen to best advantage at the beach of the Grande Jatte.
After the coy voyeurs perform their routine blushes
at the nudely refashioned Temple de l'Amour,
they pose at all their accustomed spots,
as still and stiff and static as the models of Seurat.
There, these *stoïques* of Paris stare across the Seine.
Perhaps they envy the *prolétaires* bathing on the other side,
their laughter and their skin.
Or perhaps their affectless attention is drawn by — by what?
Nemo surfacing in the sun?
Can, possibly, they comprehend what the *Nautilus* portends?
Do they really think the island's temple won't soon revert to Mars?

Confusion of Perception

Why are sugar and stress
both expressed by Sigma?
And why is holiness
signified by stigma?
Look into an abyss—
maybe you'll see Darkness
or maybe find a Nest.
Meanings make enigma.

By Way of Earth and Bone

O ye bags of burlap
with balloons and sponges stuffed,
and packets of excrement
and old bones for the bloodhounds—
someone has stabbed
your middle, your top
to let in and then let out
the noise and the moisture,
the dirt and beauty,
of the green blue golden
Earth beyond your shed.
But what game you have bagged!
What species lost!
O Burlap
Who gavest thou dominion?

Her Warnings, Her Fate

The man with too many fingers
married the one with too much gold.
And the two of them were drinkers,
and they liked their gin tonics cold.

Her sister's warnings against his grasping hands
fell like waves of surf between the grains of sand.
Her mother's sermons on passions and liquor
failed to make the flame of her candle flicker.

The man with too many fingers
married the one with too much gold.
They sang along to old singles
as he loaded his .44's.

Her father pointed to his penchant for guns
but none of Dad's batters could score any runs.
His worried warnings about those grasping hands
fell like waves of surf between the grains of sand.

The man with too many fingers
married the one with too much gold,
and together they grew wrinkled
and their love never lost its hold.

Crane

—You gray manygated bird,
O killer of murderous snakes.
Listen! to these hungry doomed soldati
trying to keep their spirits up,
these cold, these weary, these hungry doomed soldati
singing their mournful "Zhuravli"*

*At times I feel the casualties
of battle never really died.
Their buried flags are flying V's.
They became cranes unfurled in flight.*

As they ravage their way blindly
through the countryside and out,
these cold, these weary, these hungry, these doomed
sing their paean to the fallen of their Great Patriotic War
not knowing they are singing their own prophecy.

*The wars of long ago are not
so long ago. The cranes still cry.
The air is filled with fire and shot.
Low moans and shrieks shatter the skies.*

Crane — you listen and recall.
Kyiv had indeed once been freed
by their very grandpas.
But now they seek to reenslave.
History revels in irony.

*The cranes still flap in formation
through the twilights and through the mists.
A line break, an indication
I'll fill that vacancy we missed.*

Crane — you stand for freedom,
honor, prestige, supreme military dignity.
Sorrow for a motherland.
And longevity! But also sacrifice.

And so the day will surely come
when I take my place in the gap
and you'll hear my birdwings hum from
where I left you there on the map.

Crane — you sound your trumpet.
Stand tall and upright in Dnieperland.
Be like your cousin cranes,
the guardians of Midir's gates
who stripped away the courage
of any battlebound warrior
who passed their way.
But feel pity for the soldati
even as you punish them,
and even as they devolve
into deserters or barbarians.

*"Cranes," popular Russian song by Rasul Gamzatov and Yan Frenkels

Rainbows and Lightning Bolts

Enoch lived a year of years,
his eyes were a year of hours.
With time and sight he explored
the World beyond the world.

The mountains sliced Wind into plurals.
Polar pus distilled into rivers and seas.
Humanity emerged from rain and earth.

But then angelbastards
graced with greed and lust
polluted the pure, pure mud.
And an acquired shortage
of honest wisdom worship
separated humanity from Heaven.

In the expulsion from Eden
evil was not abandoned there.
Evil became humanity's pet
and humanity's pampered jewel.

Heat and cold armwrestle
their way through eternities,
while sun and moon,
those swollen stars,
exemplify their standards.

And then the Great Extinction,
a missed opportunity —
unwise Noah and progeny,
not returned to mud,
perpetuated creation's mistake.

Can original sinpride be ever unlearned?
New rainbows are forged
in the lightning bolt's factory.
Births and sunsets share their source.

Act of Love

We perform nightly on the world's smallest stage.
Rehearsed improvisation sweetens the play,
but lines and choreography never change.

Quantum Relativity

and beginnings end and ends begin.
eternities move ahead and back.

our present is the time to butcher
before the now determines our fast.

in the spot between gone and again
all whitenesses contain shades of black.

some poets remember the future
and other poets create the past.

Retired Doesn't Mean Tired Again

no phone no keys no watch
no schedule to keep
just time to think deep thoughts

or go to sleep

VIII

Sans entrée

A key that lost its lock,
I'm the one your memory forgot.

But I still remember
the many yous that once simmered
in imagination
like savory soups at the brunch
buffet. Which would you be,
the bisque, the chowder, the puree?
Your meats, beyond compare,
paradox of welldone and rare!
The romance of hors d'euvres,
breads, appetizers, drinks, desserts!
The anguish of dressings,
the conclusions of all good things.

We passed in constant halls
but you never opened your door.

A Modest Saga

Would I were that arctic skald
whose songs of ice, flood, and fire
he sang in your Valhalla
had ignited your desires.
His poems were vikings
that left your towers burning.
Instead, these runic writings
get drowned in their dry yearnings.

Dawn Children

1. BADGE

Laughter
is to
my daughter

as

rafter
is to
white water.

2. A DAY

A day short of forever.
The unread poem unwritten yet
and Mandalay sits there like a sunrise.

Drive

Never to lust
is a waste
of life
but
to just
be lust's slave
is never wise.
Lust is the drive
in the gear
and tires
that
screams "strive"
to the wheels
of winning cars,
but too much stick,
too much gas,
too much
risk
can wreck,
turn to ash,
what once was rush.

Beware

the shape within the shade,
the cape that hides the blade,
the distraction, the dodge,
the artful camouflage.

Shed light on dark matter.
Maya must be shattered.

Opposing Octaines: A Diptych

And thus have we survived Time's constriction:
Our birthright has yielded to castration,
imagination consigned to fiction,
the possible straitened since Creation.
Our regular Sunday crucifixions,
augmented by dances and cremations,
reduced by constraints and interdictions
to meaningless recreations.

***

My universe expanding
from a drop of hydrogen.
My world blessed by dawns and springs,
rainbowed by imaginings.
Any tomorrow has wings.
This is why I dance and sing:
Ending joins with beginning
every closure with an in.

Drought

It's dusty and it's dry,
my old grassy field —
I can't lay there anymore.
But the River
has bared her thighs.
Her long brown banks
burn.
Her parched navel beckons.

Harvest

Petals of platelets flee
the husks of skin and hair
emptied of liberty,
leaving our garden bare.

No gardener was maimed,
we were only sleeping.
While we were entertained
the mob stole our freedom.

As our shining Red Sea
flows among the tombstones
engraved with guarantees,
grinning skulls and crossbones
of grim politicos
inspire the patriots,
deluded, and yobos
to rampage and riot
behind the strobe smokescreen
of media disguises.

Smug pundits smile and preen
and replace sense with lies.

Under the loud bleachers
our scarlet roses fled
while the unbowed preachers
trampled our sweet seed bed.

Hope, Love, God

We Meat Creatures
are easily damaged,
prone to age and spoilage.
Not understanding
our habitat
or each other
or ourselves,
we survive
by hiding from fact.
Reason by emotion
is compromised,
and honor by opportunity.
We are content
to admire our meat
in those mirrors we devised
to fool us to believe
in distorted reverses.
After all, inevitability
is actually optional
in the cosmography
of our minds.

Alchemic connection
to some other's meat
justifies our crimes.
We know an impossible entity
of infinite opposites
exerts omnipotent
omniscient allness
to the exclusive end
of salvaging us from our natures.
We mistake for a miracle
the mirage the mirrors reveal.

Gondwanaland

This weak hiker
defeated by heat and the hills
wonders:

Could any cartographer
have encompassed your entire,
the diptych topography
of your shrouds and celebrations?
—any climatologist
comprehended your sunshine
and your thunders?
—or philosopher
have devised a system
that resolved
your paradox?

Then, how could I,
your own layman with skin in the game
have ever
composed your spread sheet?

Instant Bristlecone

Not like a loaf gone stale.

Not a burdened bristlecone,
One
ring mOre,
and then
anOther.

And not like barn paint
afading from bright youth.

Instead,
    suddenly.

Every meter's a marathon.
Organs collapsed, woodwinds muted.
Every face lost to dust and smoke—
halved or quartered, memories absconded.
And lovers' beauties
knotted and gnarled
by sO many rings.

To Be Savored at a Later Date

It takes a long time to get old.
25,000 mayfly lives.
A million molecular extinctions.
When at last I finish the course
the doctors will award me a diploma,
my certificate of achievement,
and the papers will publish
my C.V. and my survivors.
And for a few days
everyone will say nice things about me.

IX

My Lovers, A Puzzle

I believed love would transcend all fashion
and outlast all time and surpass all distance,

memory would always recall the "once"
even if that moment's lovers would change.

Memory, I thought, forged eternal chains.
Now, none of the jigsaw pieces will match.

They repose, inert, scattered, unattached,
though I recall some names, some body parts.

I can't make out their shadows in the dark
though I know they once lit up my passion.

Made to Order

The poets in the garret, the poets in the pulpit, the poets in the harem, the poets in the forum, the poets at the lectern, the poetsaseditors, the poets in the board room, the poets in uniform

They all actuate the dancer, model the romantic, command the murder words, provoke the murder hordes, invoke the deity, model the fealty, incite blood and honor, inspire holy bombers.

That's what poets do.

My Kireji, My Coke

Haijin, I had ordered your lines
when you uttered the cutting word.
Then you withdrew, O Addiction,
leaving me with all withdrawal.

Best Advice I Can Give

Beware the rustlers in the weeds,
be they beasts or be they thieves.

Beware comehithers in the dark.
They exist as both bait and shark.
They're the lure and you're the mark.

But also know what is good:
Learn to sort the can't from the could.

Brahma and Shiva are the Same

Creation and destruction share a pulse.
Given the infinities of time and space,
everything takes turns as everything else.
Trees become jewels at a diamond's pace.
The birds used to be dinosaurs;
mountains, plains; and deserts, flowers.
The Eves were made of galaxy atoms
after doing their stint as orchids,
and constellations became Adams,
while apples once were arachnids.

Communing

I forgot how to speak Nature
and must relearn the dialects
of savanna stone sky sand sea
and listen when Wind whispers.
I must don my shoes of creek,
tiger, worm, and squirrel my way
through birdsong woods,
let grasses swallow my toes.

Flower me with wonder.
Bring back my Wild.

Rule Under Law!

Riding my circuit in the bayou
I wondered what made the mamasan
tout your value and assets so much.
But I understood why when I saw you,
O, titular Queen of Amazons!

And then you dubbed me the Hanging Judge
after we retired to our chamber.
The unthroned queen and the disrobed judge
weighed majesty and jurisprudence
and ruled that no appeal from danger
and no loss of honor or of blood
would overrule our love's innocence.

In the regular session to come,
accepting only the guilty pleas,
we presided over the night court.
The scale of justice under our thumbs,
we sentenced love's arsonists and thieves
to life at hard labor, no parole.

Come the Revolution

Which among you will bring sandwiches?
And who'll organize the selfies?
Which manifesto would you execute?
"The sky must be purged if the earth is to prevail!"
"The earth must be buried for Heaven to reveal!"
Which Utopia would you provoke?
Which of the pasts should be banned?
But don't be the freak hot on the runway
or the gangster in church,
don't be the priest caught in the whore house,
or banker man in the lineup.

The Mare's Breaking In

Wanting the beads and the choirs,
she took the veil and cincture.
But inside the now
she regrets the vow,
since accepting the saddle
imposed spurs, bit, and bridle.

White Dwarf Eulogy

My sweet sweet sun.
Every day you sport your saffron robe
and leaven my starch with your butter.
You honey my room by daylight
and bower it by night, flower and feed me
all the year.
If you were gone
even the moon would
disappea

*

I recall writing this one
and working another two
when the night was black like tar,
hours before the morning's light
would color sky with new dyes.
We can't look long at the sun,
but you're so unlike the sun.

You said you wanted cashews
to refill your empty jar,
a healthful snack at midnight
for better sleep by and by.
I, instead, proposed almonds.
And I can't help but see you
though I cannot look at you.

So you got into your car.
You waved, turned on the headlights,
switched your beam from low to high,
and gave the engine the gun.
Out of the driveway you flew.
Though the sun's just one more star,
you're my only superstar.

I resumed work on my writes
and lost track of time and sky.
With no warning, you were gone.
Blackness never became blue,
and your nearness went afar.
The sun hides away at night,
you're with me through all the nights.

That was when I learned to cry
and forgot a race is won
through union with a new crew.
I can't accept that life's char
can help me cherish the white.
In the end the sun will die.
To me, not ever will you die

Paradoxical, Isn't It?

Nothing demarcates order like death.
We the living are the anarchy.

Passion accrues psychic debt.
Mankind's defined by love and anger.

We exalt and diminish heroes
and cherish and ignore our mothers.

We worship at the shrine of ego
and yet sacrifice self for others.

Last Wishes

Bury me not in the air
like a banner on a mast.
I want no saluters when I'm gone.
And not in water, not in earth,
where bones transition to brass,
and bios become plaques.
And don't bury me in fire.
The soul will turn to ash,
and memories to embers.
Let an end start a dawn
as uselessness gains worth.
Present my corpse to science.

X

Absent Pasts, Mnemonic Futures

1. Barbs Without Strand

Uplit by tragedy
or success, the Event Times
are the pix captured in strongest focus.
Mundane times between leave no traces.

2. Ties Without Track

Mapped by geography
I recollect the Place Times.
Those memories cluster like galaxies.
The times between, black matter vacuums.

3. Knots Without String

Channeled by media
I recall Pop Culture Times.
Memories, programmed archipelagoes,
the times between silent, imageless.

4. Bulbs Without Wire

Grouped by society
I recall People Times.
Those memories are linked like oases.
The times between lack names and faces.

Aces and 8s: The Deaths of Poetry

18 shots at the white horse
and nothing for it but remorse

in a dune buggy on the isle of fire
an end to acquisition and desire

cooped, ravin' in another man's suit
selfresolution of mystery and truth

missolonghi's profligatemartyr's heart
selfexcess that altruism's waters part

boston quick head unrisen in the oven
thought abandoned by creation and love

falangist bullets spat in altacar
the past of the future unmarked

a disemboweling retrosamurai
everunanswered search for why

rafting across the Sambre, killed by duty
the always link to waste and beauty

dakar rule reminiscing 20 years on
poetry's incompatibility with power.

Reflection

My fate is a matter of taste,
will, opportunity, and ties.

Existence can be unfair.

A pilot pushes for the horizon
or bigger payload.

Some folks *want* to be honest.

My only choice is to be the virgin
or the volcano.

Most of us wish to be lawless.

Whenever I look at my face
I see the liar in my eyes.

Time

Wednesday
was
the last day I ate.

Thursday,
I'm hungry.

Multipledivisionsaremeaningless,existenceremainsone.

Bloom's *Kama Sutra*, new edition

To the garden of harlots I pilgrimage again.
"Hey, Bud."
The rival queens of the bed compete for attention and agency.
"Pick me, pick me."
Their perfumes, their costume hyperbole, all tended for effect. Their gloss and glitter lipstick, their soft and tender feel.
"I just know you came to sniff my genitals. As usual."
I contemplate paradise in every connate petal. The throats, the limbs.
"Why don't you take me home with you?" The spiked heels, the hiked-up miniskirts and stuffed brassieres.
"Oh, Rose, everyone knows you're wilting already. So, Mister, take me instead. You won't regret."
I blush — the brash sunflowers are selfing again. Shameless exhibitionists!
"Hey, Bud!"
The blossoms' bosoms sway like ecstasy while stems swivel and gyrate. The anthor sacs split boldly open, the pistils expose their sticky tips, their fine tiny hairs. Oh, my!
"My nectar is sweet and yours for the tasting."
Their scents, their scents, I do believe they're engineered purely to test my feigned reticence.
"I do bouquets."
Though I confess, after all these years, I savor their style still, I am aware that there is a stigma attached.
But, this time, nevertheless, I choose to cruise the hothouse nearby. Rumor has it that the orchids are in gametophyte.

The Firing Squad

Those diligent gardeners of fascism
—they plant themselves
in their appointed rows
and finger their potting tools.

They commence to prune.
They pursue their weeding task.

Their mechanical motions
are repetitive, frequent,
predictable.

And squinting is unnecessary.
Individual aim is irrelevant.
Collective action is pure.

But the roses that sprout
from every bullet hole
will germinate tomorrow's blight.
And the multiflora will supplant
the cultivation and the gardeners.

Impressario

Life After Life was the climax
for Jesus of Nazareth.
Before revealing his magic
he rehearsed on Lazarus.

He minutely choreographed
the entire threeday event
and timed the showpiece perfectly
to take advantage of Lent.

The spectacle had everything:
pageantry, special effects,
dramatic memorable lines,
and passage from Death to Next!

Of course it played to mixed reviews,
loved or hated by the critics.
Some lauded the instant classic
and others labeled it schtick.

When They Love Us Not

When the ones we want to love us
leave no doubt we've been left behind,
should we loll about, scavengers
of leftovers lying around?
Or should we collate our losses
like alarmed lieutenants behind
the lines, wannabe avengers
of honor lost on our naked rout?

Crock

In a minute second
in the second minute
of the year—

I did not notice
that the gods
of my ears, my eyes,
my hands, my mind
took their sudden leave.

I could see
no scythe, no valkyrie,
no blue myriadeyed ram,
no acrobats or clowns
to remind me
how experience
is so fleeting.
No feathertilting scales.

The air merely escaped
from a closed jar
to a larger atmosphere.

After Death, What?

If reincarnation be real
I'll return as someone else,
and if resurrection be true
I'll just come back as myself.

It might be a grand adventure,
refitting an ancient sloop
christened *The Comeback Kid's Return,*
sailing to exotic ports.

But there is much to recommend
the familiarity
of a comfortable prospect
from my worn house by the sea.

Life after life may be a lie.
The end may be the end.
Some day would have no tomorrow.
No avatars. No Heaven.

Afterwords

A Cento*

"There must be some way out of here," said the joker to the thief, "There's too much confusion, I can't get no relief. Businessmen, they drink my wine, plowmen dig my earth, none of them along the line know what any of it is worth."

"No reason to get excited," the thief, he kindly spoke, "There are many here among us who feel that life is but a joke. But you and I, we've been through that, and this is not our fate, so let us not talk falsely now, the hour is getting late."

All along the watchtower, princes kept the view while all the women came and went, barefoot servants, too. Outside in the distance a wildcat did growl, two riders were approaching, the wind began to howl. Well, I dreamed I saw the knights in armor coming, saying something about a queen. There were peasants singing and drummers drumming, and the archer split the tree. There was a fanfare blowing to the sun that was floating on the breeze. Look at Mother Nature on the run in the current century.

I was lying in a burned-out basement with the full moon in my eyes. I was hoping for replacement when the sun burst through the sky. There was a band playing in my head and I felt like getting high. I was thinking about what a friend had said. I was hoping it was a lie.

I dreamed I saw the silver spaceships flying in the yellow haze of the sun, There were children crying and colors flying all around the chosen ones. All in a dream, all in a dream, the loading had begun. They were flying Mother Nature's silver seed to a new home in the sun.

*Bob Dylan, "All Along the Watch Tower," Neil Young, "After the Gold Rush"

Elvis, Oedipus, and Akhnaton

Three wizened kings sip and swap their yarns
about hound dogs, a sphinx, and the sun.

Confusions among daughters, wives, and moms
seem commonplace, they wisely agree.

"Is fate how we see, or how we're seen?"
"Beauty is deformity's trophy."

"Am I isolated by greatness?"
"Have I passed or have I failed the test?"

"Did crowd gravity make me weightless,
or did I fly up in levity?"

"Just grin against grim adversity,
so you won't end fat, blind, and defaced."

"Shall music, honor, or religion
yet bridge our world's fissures and schisms?"

"Will legend persist against reason?"
"It matters not. Let's down another!"

"To all our followers and lovers."
"To all the memories we gather."

Elvis, Oedipus, and Akhnaton,
three wizened kings sip and swap their yarns.

A Dodge City Nativity

Marshall made the perfect badge by
adding salvation to danger,
and in all his gunfights he lays
fire down first, and with unmatched eye.

The needed balance between grace
and punishment was childfragile
when the HighHanded Old Stranger
brought his card sharp skill into play.

While dealing, his hands were agile.
He fast established the game changer.
He also sleeved the highest ace
to assure he held the edge, aye!

Marshall sent posses of angels
to greet the shepherds and magi
as they encountered the starblaze
and miracle of the manger.

Cord for Lifting, For Lynching

The divers and the bathers,
like misers and savers,
are akin but not twins.

Sometimes, optimists are pessimists
and, at times, pessimists optimists.

High even in our depths,
we optimists can await
the fullness of time
since precious hope clothes
our minds with concern.

But, crying as we laugh,
we pessimists contemplate
the awfulness of time.
A vicious rope chokes,
we wind and we turn.

Inner shamans
shape our natures
with their visions
of our futures.

We're jammin' in our band
as famine eats our land.

The Calligrapher Writes the Landscape

The rain's crowquill paints ink across pigeongray parchment sky and draft indelibly
themselves upon an eager gravid ground

and the sins and memories, and hopes and charities, that take root, grafted into
the earth, remain ensoiled past the droughts and floods to come.

The Parts Left Out May Be as Important as the Parts Left In: An Illustration

—Duane Vorhees

About the Author

You're such a sad, searching, deepthinking erudite, gifted brilliant, silty cynical guy! Your intriguing poetry sucks me in every time.

—Arlene Corwin

Your works will be studied long after we're all gone.

—Rashid Pelpuo

Your work here is incredibly original…. Some of these poems touch me — and touch me deeply…. When they work for me, they work incredibly well. I envy your wordplay and originality…. I cannot say I understand all of your poems, such is your depth and erudition, but there's an awful lot I like. I am a little jealous that you have such a playful muse, and for you it seems she gives and gives and gives; but tonight I will sip my frosty beer knowing that I can ski faster than you.

—Peter Wodarz

I loved your poetry, spinetingling insights actually…. Love poetry that is emotive and makes me think.

—Amrita Valan

It is such a pleasure to read your poetry…. I love the subject, style, phrasing and imagery of each poem.

—Strider Mark Jones

Far more than the typical café stanzas, each entry is ablaze with wisdom and beautifully brutal. This is the kind of raw and orphic poetry we've been missing since Byron, or Bukowski. I read and reread your poems, and I have to tell you that they're the best pieces of verse I've read in a while. Very engrossing, and they left me inspired! Enough so that they have me writing poetry again. These poems you've crafted are like torch fire on the far side of the fog. I hope to find my way to where your pen stands waiting.... It was a restorative read, for as I read I would stop to grab my notebook and pen poems of my own.... It takes a remarkable poet to motivate one to rouse from a protracted period of grief. What a conflagration courses through these, your years of looking back.... Yours is indeed one of the most genuine, and experimental, voices I've encountered hitherto.... I see so much anecdote in your writing. You've lived these poems, haven't you?

—Dennis Williamson

I am constantly amazed at how much you know and how you weave skillful poems around it all.

—Beth Weaver

Magical words. Your poetry is worth reading over and over.

—Sugar Zedna

I always delight in your naughtiness, word play, multiple entendre, but also see travel and multiple interpretations of life's issues along with a genuine love and appreciation and respect for the language.

—Dave Norris

Unscrew the doors themselves from their jambs! Behold the universe! A drooling idiot! Feast on it with your jaws! Dance in your mask, we're watching. I want to see you fire the gun again, at the sky, so I can laugh. In that sound you made in laughing; I don't know what it was. What are you laughing at, Duane?....We're going to ban you, I promise. We'll put you in the cage! We'll record your voice! Your gift will be to the king, and the sentence is, that you will have to keep giving it!

—Robin Wyatt Dunn

www.ingramcontent.com/pod-product-compliance
Lightning Source LLC
Chambersburg PA
CBHW081429070526
44586CB00020B/2534